CHRIST
IS
RISEN

The Passion and the Resurrection
of Jesus Christ

With Icons and Scriptures from the Orthodox Study Bible
for Children and Adults

Written and Illustrated by

Maria Athanasiou

To all the children of God

Acknowledgments

Special thanks to the following for the blessings and their theological guidance:
Rev. Fr. Sarantis Loulakis of Saint Markella Greek Orthodox Church,
Wantagh, New York
Rev. Fr. Nicholas Soteropoulos of Saint Petros the Apostle Greek Orthodox
Church, Bronx, New York
Special thanks for her artistic advice: My talented daughter, Elizabeth Soteropoulos

The Orthodox Study Bible

The English Gospel text used is from 'The Holy and Sacred Gospel', and the English text of the Acts of the Apostles and Epistles is used from 'The Apostolos', both by Holy Cross Press, Brookline, MA. The English Old Testament text is taken from the Revised Standard Version of the Bible.

The Revised Standard Version of the Bible is copyrighted 1946, 1952, 1971, and 1973 by the Division of Christian Education of the National Council of the Churches of Christ in the U.S.A. and used by permission.

Print information available on the last page

Rev. date: 03/26/2019

To order additional copies of this book, contact:
Xlibris
1-888-795-4274
www.Xlibris.com
Orders@Xlibris.com

The Face of Jesus Christ

It was written long ago that the Messiah must suffer and die and come back to life again to give whoever believes in Him redemption and eternal life. This is the story of the Holy Week, the last week of the life of Jesus on earth.

For it is the God who commanded light to shine out of darkness, who has shone in our hearts to give the light of the knowledge of the glory of God in the face of Jesus Christ. **2 Corinthians 4:6**

Jesus Is the Resurrection and the Life

On Saturday before the feast of the Passover, Jesus with His disciples went to Bethany in Judea, up on the slope of the Mount of Olives, to the house of His good friend, Lazarus. The sisters of Lazarus, Mary and Martha, were in tears because Lazarus had died four days ago, and he was buried. Jesus was overcome with sadness, and He wept with them. Martha said to Him, "Lord, if you were here, my brother would not have died.

Jesus said to her, "Your brother will rise again."

Martha said to Him, "I know that he will rise again in the resurrection at the last day."

Jesus said to her, "I am the resurrection and the life. He who believes in Me, though he may die, he shall live. And whoever lives and believes in Me shall never die. Do you believe this?"

She said to Him, "Yes, Lord, I believe that You are the Christ, the Son of God, who is to come into the world." **John 11:23-27**

Jesus brought Lazarus back to life with His Divine Power and changed the sadness into joy. All who were present and eyewitnesses of the raising of Lazarus believed that Jesus Christ was the Son of God, the Messiah, the Savior whom they expected to save them from the cruelty of the Romans; but when the high priest and the Pharisees saw the multitude of people following Jesus, they were very afraid of losing their power. They envied Jesus and started to look for a way to kill Him.

Palm Sunday

On Sunday, it was time for Jesus to leave Bethany and go to Jerusalem, two miles away, for the feast of the Passover. Great joy was in the air. Hundreds of people who loved Him and had witnessed His wonders and His miracles were following Him, shouting and singing praises as He entered Jerusalem through the Golden Gate.

The next day a great multitude that had come to the feast, when they heard that Jesus was coming to Jerusalem, took branches of palm trees and went out to meet Him, and cried out: *"Hosanna! 'Blessed is He who comes in the name of the LORD! "The King of Israel!"* **John 12:12-13**

On the Sunday before Easter, it is a tradition of the Orthodox Church to prepare palm crosses to honor Jesus, in remembrance of His triumphant entrance into Jerusalem and of the cross He endured to save our souls.

The *palm* represents His glorious coming, and the *cross* represents His passion.
The *palm branches* were rewards for champions and winners of wars.
The *Golden Gate* is the most beautiful of Jerusalem's gates, located on the eastern wall. It is also known as the *Gate of Eternal Life*.

The Lord in the Temple

Immediately after Jesus came to Jerusalem, He was in the temple praying and teaching about God, the Creator, and His kingdom in heaven. Since very early in the morning, crowds of people were coming to hear Him speak. Jesus told them that He is the Son of Man, which means that He is the Son of God, and they believed in Him.

Jesus also warned them to beware of the Pharisees and the scribes, for they were hypocrites and dishonest. Many times He challenged them with parables or small stories. Parables require special attention and spiritual ears to be understood because they have a hidden meaning.

Now when the chief priests and Pharisees heard His parables, they perceived that He was speaking of them. But when they sought to lay hands on Him, they feared the multitudes, because they took Him for a prophet. **Matthew 21:45-46**

The Gift of Eternal Life

On Thursday, Jerusalem was crowded with people for the Passover. Jesus with His disciples went in the "upper room," where Peter and John had prepared their Passover lamb meal. When they all were around the table, Jesus told them that He was happy to have this meal with them, but He was also sad because this was His last supper before His suffering. He added that one of them would betray Him. Judas knew it was him. He quickly ran out in the darkness of the night and headed for the Pharisees because he had agreed to betray the Lord to them for thirty silver dollars.

And as they were eating, Jesus took bread, blessed and broke it, and gave it to the disciples and said, "Take, eat; this is My body." Then He took the cup, and gave thanks, and gave it to them, saying, "Drink from it, all of you. For this is **My blood of the new covenant**, which is shed for many for the remission of sins. But I say to you, I will not drink of this fruit of the vine from now on until that day when I drink it new with you in My Father's kingdom." **Matthew 26:26-29**

Holy Communion is a gift of our Lord. The body and blood of our Lord Jesus Christ lead us to salvation and redemption of our souls.

Eucharist means offering thanks in Greek. Christ offered thanks to God the Father. We offer thanks to God for His precious gift of eternal life.

On *Holy Thursday*, we reenact and commemorate His last supper and that first Holy Communion in the "upper room."

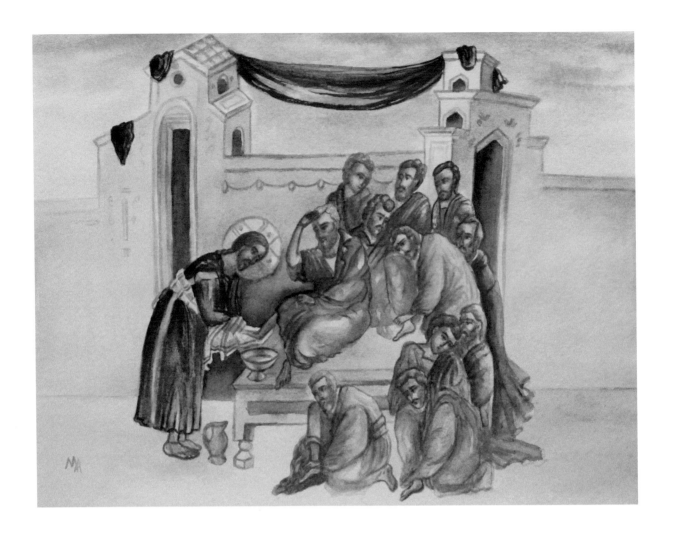

A Lesson of Humility

After the supper ended, Jesus took a towel and a basin with water and washed His disciples' feet, showing them by example how to be humble.

So when He had washed their feet, taken His garments, and sat down again, He said to them, "Do you know what I have done to you? You call Me Teacher and Lord, and you say well, for so I am. If I then, your Lord and Teacher, have washed your feet, you also ought to wash one another's feet. For I have given you an example, that you should do as I have done to you. **John 13:12-15**

Jesus can wash away our sins and save our souls if we believe in Him.

The *Lord* is the one who has power to give life and holds the whole world in His hands.

On *Holy Wednesday* evening, faithful Christians receive holy oil, for the healing of their body and the cleansing of their soul, to prepare themselves to receive the Holy Communion on Holy Thursday.

Watch and Pray

Later that evening, Jesus and His disciples sang a hymn, and then they went outside to the Garden of Gethsemane in the Mount of Olives. Jesus took Peter, James, and John with Him and walked a little farther. He told them He was sad and scared and asked them to stay awake with Him. Jesus knew His hour had come to suffer the death on the cross. His human side was in great agony as He kneeled down to pray.

And He said, "Abba, Father, all things are possible for You. Take this cup away from Me; nevertheless, not what I will, but what You will."

Then He came and found them sleeping, and said to Peter, "Simon, are you sleeping? Could you not watch one hour? Watch and pray, lest you enter into temptation. The spirit indeed is willing, but the flesh is weak." **Mark 14:36-38**

Prayer is a communication with God that will keep us safe and away from temptation. In prayer, we thank Him, praise Him, and ask for His mercy and His grace.

Betrayed with a Kiss

And while He was still speaking, behold, a multitude; and he who was called Judas, one of the twelve, went before them and drew near to Jesus to kiss Him. But Jesus said to him, "Judas, are you betraying the Son of Man with a kiss?" **Luke 22:47-48**

The kiss was a sign for them to recognize who Jesus was; the officers of the temple arrested Jesus at once and brought Him to Caiaphas, the high priest. The disciples ran to hide, except for Peter, who followed from a distance but denied he knew Christ three times before the rooster crowed, as Jesus had said.

The scribes and the elders accused Jesus with false accusations. They tortured Him all night, and in the morning, they asked Him if He is the Christ, the Son of God. When Jesus answered yes, they wanted Him killed and brought Him to the Roman governor, Pontius Pilate, because he only had the authority to sentence anyone to death. They said that Jesus was misleading people from Galilee through all Judea, teaching them that He is Christ the King.

Pilate asked Christ, "Are you the King of the Jews?"

And He answered him, "You have said so."

But Pilate found nothing to condemn Jesus to death and sent Him to Herod, a Galilean judge, who was also in Jerusalem at that time. Herod asked Jesus many questions but found nothing to condemn Him and sent Him back to Pilate.

Every Wednesday is a day of strict fast to honor our Lord, in remembrance of the day He was betrayed.

A Crown of Thorns

Then the soldiers of the governor took Jesus into the Praetorium and gathered the whole garrison around Him. And they stripped Him and put a **scarlet robe** on Him. When they had twisted a crown of thorns, they put it on His head, and a reed in His right hand. And they bowed the knee before Him and mocked Him, saying, "Hail, King of the Jews! **Matthew 27:27-29**

Holy Thursday is the night we place wreaths of flowers on the cross as an expression of love for His sacrifice, His crown of glory.

Golgotha

Pilate told the chief priests and the rulers that neither he nor Herod found anything wrong concerning Jesus. The custom was to release one prisoner before Passover, and Pilate wanted to release Jesus Christ because he knew they wanted to kill Him out of envy; so he offered them Barabbas, who was a thief and a murderer. But the crowd, bribed by the Pharisees, insisted that he should release Barabbas and crucify Jesus. So Pilate released Barabbas and delivered Jesus to be crucified after he tortured Him.

Jesus had to carry His cross through the streets of Jerusalem to Golgotha. He was bleeding from the beatings and needed help to carry the heavy cross.

Now as they led Him away, they laid hold of a certain man, Simon a Cyrenian, who was coming from the country, and on him they laid the cross that he might bear it after Jesus. **Luke 23:26**

Golgotha was also called the place of the Skull Hill. That was the place of execution.

Sorrowful Mother

The Virgin Mary was following the Lord as He was carrying His cross up the hill to Golgotha. Her tender heart was in pain as she saw Him bleeding and falling. Her Son, the Lamb of God, was led to be slaughtered by the Roman soldiers, and she remembered the words of Simeon in the temple on the Presentation Day, when he said, "Behold, this Child is destined for the fall and rising of many in Israel, and for a sign which will be spoken against (yes, a sword will pierce through your own soul also), that the thoughts of many hearts may be revealed." **Luke 2:34-35**

Simeon was a devout man in Jerusalem. God had revealed to him that he would not die before he saw Christ the Messiah. The day Joseph and Mary brought the Child Christ to the temple on Presentation Day, Simeon, led by the Spirit, was there and recognized Jesus as Lord.

The *Lord* is *God, Kyrios* in Greek, the one who gives life.

Lord, Remember Me

It was at the place of the skull that they nailed Jesus on the cross. The sign "Jesus Christ, King of the Jews" was inscribed over the cross of Christ, as Pilate ordered. Two thieves were hanged on either side of Him. The one on the left told Jesus, "If you are the Christ, save yourself and us." But the criminal on His right rebuked the disrespectful thief, saying to him, "Don't you have any respect for God? We have sinned and deserve this punishment, but this Man has done nothing wrong."

Then he said to Jesus, "Lord, remember me when You come into Your kingdom."

And Jesus said to him, "Assuredly, I say to you, today you will be with Me in Paradise." **Luke 23:42-43**

The only road to Paradise is our Lord Jesus Christ.
The prayer for every Christian is "Lord, remember me in Your kingdom."

The Amazing Love of God

Jesus knew He had completed His work on earth. Concerning His enemies, He said, "Father, forgive them, for they do not know what they are doing." Then He said, "It is finished," and gave up His spirit.

It was Friday afternoon when Jesus died. There was a big earthquake, and darkness covered the face of the earth. The curtain of the Temple was torn, and the centurion said, "This was truly the Son of God."

Jesus accepted to die to destroy death and save our souls. His passionate love for us is amazing. He suffered and died for you and for me so that we may have eternal life in the kingdom of heaven.

In a conversation with Nicodemos, Jesus had said, "For God so loved the world that He gave His only begotten Son, that whoever believes in Him should not perish but have everlasting life". **John 3:16**

Friday is the preparation day before the Jewish Sabbath. It is a day of strict fast in remembrance of the passion and death of our Lord.

The Burial

Joseph of Arimathea, a counsel member who was seeking the kingdom of God, was a secret disciple of Jesus because he was afraid of the Jews. He went to Pilate and asked permission to receive the body of Christ. Together with Nicodemos, a Pharisee who had first come to visit Jesus by night, Joseph took the body of Jesus down from the cross.

Now when evening had come, there came a rich man from Arimathea, named Joseph, who himself had also become a disciple of Jesus. This man went to Pilate and asked for the body of Jesus. Then Pilate commanded the body to be given to him. **Matthew 27:57-58**

A *disciple* is a follower and a student of serious commitment and self-sacrifice. The disciples of Jesus were hiding because they were afraid for their lives. Without fear, His secret disciples by night requested the body of Jesus, and Pilate granted it.

The Tomb of Jesus

When Joseph had taken the body, he wrapped it in a clean linen cloth, and laid it in his new tomb which he had hewn out of the rock; and he rolled a large stone against the door of the tomb, and departed. And Mary Magdalene was there, and the other Mary, sitting opposite the tomb. **Matthew 27:59-61**

And Caiaphas posted guards around the tomb to prevent the apostles from coming and stealing the body.

Christ Is Risen

Very early on Sunday morning, the Virgin Mary with Mary Magdalene and Salome came to the tomb with spices, and they found it empty. An angel shining brightly in white was there, and he spoke to them.

But he said to them, "Do not be alarmed. You seek Jesus of Nazareth, who was crucified. **He is risen**! He is not here. See the place where they laid Him. But go, tell His disciples, and Peter, that He is going before you into Galilee; there you will see Him, as He said to you."

So they went out quickly and fled from the tomb, for they trembled and were amazed. And they said nothing to anyone, for they were afraid. **Mark 16:6-8**

Sunday is the Resurrection day, the day of the Lord, the first day of the week.

Kyriaki means Sunday in Greek, from *Kyrios* which means "Lord." On Sunday, the Lord's Day, we give honor and praise to God because He gave us new life eternal.

Jesus Is Alive

The Virgin Mary, Mary Magdalene, and the disciples of Jesus Christ were eyewitnesses to His resurrection. They saw Him many times from the day of His resurrection until the day He ascended into heaven to be with God the Father.

Now when He rose early on the first day of the week, He appeared first to Mary Magdalene, out of whom He had cast seven demons. She went and told those who had been with Him, as they mourned and wept. **Mark 16:9-10**

The Stranger on the Road to Emmaus

Later that same Sunday, Jesus appeared for the second time to Cleopas and Luke as they were walking, but they did not recognize Him right away. They thought He was a stranger. They were very impressed with Him because He quoted many Scriptures to them. It was getting dark, and when they reached the house of Cleopas, they invited the stranger in for dinner. It was at the dinner table that they recognized Him, when He broke the bread and gave it to them; but then He disappeared, and they were suddenly alone.

Now behold, two of them were traveling that same day to a village called Emmaus, which was seven miles from Jerusalem. And they talked together of all these things which had happened. So it was, while they conversed and reasoned that Jesus Himself drew near and went with them. But their eyes were restrained, so that they did not know Him. **Luke 24:13-16**

Peace Be With You

On the evening of that same Sunday, Jesus appeared to His disciples. They were all gathered in a room with locked doors because they were afraid of the Jews. He greeted them with the resurrection greeting, "Peace be with you," and He showed them His hands and His feet and asked them for something to eat. Thomas was not with them that day, and when they told him that they saw the Lord, he did not believe them.

And after eight days His disciples were again inside, and Thomas with them. Jesus came, the doors being shut, and stood in the midst, and said, "Peace to you!" Then He said to Thomas, "Reach your finger here, and look at My hands; and reach your hand here, and put it into My side. Do not be unbelieving, but believing." And Thomas answered and said to Him, "My Lord and my God!"

Jesus said to him, "Thomas, because you have seen Me, you have believed. Blessed are those who have not seen and yet have believed." **John 20:26-29**

The Sea of Galilee

Jesus appeared again to His disciples at the Sea of Galilee. They saw Him standing by the shore early one morning, when they were coming back from an all-night fishing trip. They had caught no fish that night. But Jesus told them to throw their net at the right side of the boat, and when they did, they caught many fish.

Simon Peter went up and dragged the net to land, full of large fish one hundred and fifty-three; and although there were so many, the net was not broken. **John 21:11**

When we follow Jesus and the word of God, we will always find plenty because He will guide us where it is best for us.

The Ascension

The Lord was appearing to the disciples for forty days after His resurrection. He gave them instructions to go and preach the Gospel from Jerusalem to the whole world. He promised them that He would send them the Holy Spirit, the power from on high, to enlighten and guide them.

And Jesus came and spoke to them, saying, "All authority has been given to Me in heaven and on earth. Go therefore and make disciples of all the nations, baptizing them in the name of the Father and of the Son and of the Holy Spirit, teaching them to observe all things that I have commanded you; and lo, I am with you always, even to the end of the age." Amen. **Matthew 28:18-20**

Jesus and His disciples were on the road to Bethany. There, Jesus blessed them, lifted His hands, and began to rise into the sky on a cloud to take His place on the right hand of God, His Father; and on the clouds, He shall come again in glory. We always have to be prepared, with a pure heart, for His second coming.

As part of the *sacrament of baptism*, the above Scripture from the Gospel is read.

The Day of Pentecost

In His name, Jesus instructed His apostles to teach all nations about repentance and remission of sins. He asked them to wait in Jerusalem for the Holy Spirit to descend.

When the Day of Pentecost had fully come, they were all with one accord in one place. And suddenly there came a sound from heaven, as of a rushing mighty wind, and it filled the whole house where they were sitting. Then there appeared to them divided tongues, as of fire, and one sat upon each of them. And they were all filled with the Holy Spirit and began to speak with other tongues, as the Spirit gave them utterance. **Acts 2:1-4**

Pentecost is fifty days after the Resurrection, when Jesus sent the Holy Spirit to His disciples. The church of Christ began on that day, when Peter started to preach the Gospel.

The Holy Spirit is one of the Holy Trinity.

The Gospel is the good news of salvation.

Printed in the United States
By Bookmasters